Sue Lawrence won Masterchef in 1991 and was the President of the Guild of Food Writers from 2004 to 2007. She wrote a regular column for *Scotland on Sunday* and *Scotland* magazine and was also the *Sunday Times* food columnist. She has written for *Sainsbury's Magazine*, *Woman & Home*, *Country Living* and *BBC Good Food* magazine and appears regularly on radio and television talking about Scottish food and traditions. She won the Regional Writer Glenfiddich Food and Drink Award in 2003 for her work in *Scotland on Sunday*. She is the author of *Sue Lawrence's Book of Baking*, *Scottish Kitchen*, *A Cook's Tour of Scotland* and the award-winning *Scots Cooking*.

Sue lives in Edinburgh with her husband and three children.

Praise for Sue and her previous books:
'Edinburgh's own domestic goddess – the best home-cook in the land' Elisabeth Luard, *Scotsman*

'One of my favourite cookery writers' Darina Allen

'Imaginative cooking of impeccable taste and intelligence. An exceptional book' Richard Ehrlich, *Guardian* [on *Scottish Kitchen*]

'Sue Lawrence's recipes always work. She is a particularly fine baker' Clarissa Dickson Wright

'One of the country's finest food writers' Orlando Murrin, *Daily Express*

'She is one heck of a baker – do try her muffins, cakes and shortbreads' *Sainsbury's Magazine*

'Full of inspiring recipes' *Olive* [on *Book of Baking*]

'The recipes work and the results are delicious' *Sainsbury's Magazine*

'One of the best recipe-writers in the land' Jill Dupleix, *The Times*

Also by Sue Lawrence

A Cook's Tour of Scotland
Book of Baking
Scottish Kitchen
Scots Cooking

GREAT SCOT!

RECIPES FROM SCOTLAND
CHOSEN BY SCOTLAND'S FINEST

SUE LAWRENCE

hachette
SCOTLAND

For Isabelle, dear friend since 1963, with love

First published in 2009 by HACHETTE SCOTLAND, an imprint of Hachette UK

1

Cataloguing in Publication Data is available from the British Library ISBN: 978 0 7553 6051 2

Edited by Helena Caldon
Food styling by Maxine Clark
Food photography by Alan Donaldson
Designed and typeset by Republic Productions
Printed by Mohn Media Books, Germany

Hachette Scotland's policy is to use papers that are natural, renewable and recyclable products and made from wood grown in sustainable forests. The logging and manufacturing processes are expected to conform to the environmental regulations of the country of origin.

HACHETTE SCOTLAND
An Hachette UK Company, 338 Euston Road, London NW1 3BH
www.hachettescotland.co.uk www.hachette.co.uk

Acknowledgements   x

Foreword by Ewan McGregor   xi

Introduction   1

Soups and Starters   7

Veg, Cheese and Breakfast   41

Fish   63

Meat   83

Puddings   127

Bakes   151

Index   208

Acknowledgements

Special thanks to Sir Sean Connery, for not only telephoning me to wish me well for this book, but also for making my daughter Jessica's day as she was home alone, so able to chat to this Great Scot.

Thanks to:

Anna and Bob Anderson	Andy Hall	Judi and John Matheson
Scott Begbie	Dorothy Hilsley	Rob Mitchell
Colin Campbell	Margot Hudson	Angela Morton
Jan Gaffney	Kenneth Hume	Flora and Alan Sharp
John Gordon	John Inverdale	Rory Steel
Vivienne Grant	Isabel Johnson	Rosalind Woolfson
Elisabeth, Jackie and Sue Hadden	Bea Macdonald	

And for lending props:

Joyce Clark; Norman Lee; Timothy Hardie at Rait Village Antique Centre for letting us have the antique plaids; Bob Templeman, Scottish Antiques and Arts Centre, Abernyte and Doune; and Catherine Brown for lending one of her many girdles – a peat fire girdle for the Tattie Scones.

And also a special mention to:

Jenny Brown, literary agent extraordinaire; Bob McDevitt for his publishing vision; Maxine Clark for her brilliant food styling; Alan Donaldson for his wonderful photos; Wendy McCance and Helena Caldon for their proficient editing; and all the team at CHAS, in particular to Kerry and Roslyn. The Children's Hospice Association Scotland (CHAS) is a Scottish charity established to provide hospice services in Scotland for children and young people with life-limiting conditions. A children's hospice offers professional care, practical help and emotional support to the whole family usually from the day of acceptance, to the death of their child, and beyond. For further information, please see www.chas.org.uk

Finally, to Pat, Euan, Faith and Jessica Lawrence. Thanks, as ever, for putting up with the many Highs and occasional Lows of the resident author.

Foreword
by Ewan McGregor

When Sue Lawrence first approached me to ask if I would like to be included in her book, I was absolutely delighted. Not only did it allow me the opportunity to reminisce about the delicious home-cooked food I enjoyed as a child growing up in Crieff, but it also gave me the opportunity to show my support for the Children's Hospice Association Scotland (CHAS), a wonderful Scottish charity which has a very special place in my heart.

I have so loved reading, as I'm sure will you, the tales of the food enjoyed by Scotland's 'great and good' which Sue has researched and recorded in this book.

I would like to thank everyone who contributed and gave their time to talk to Sue and share their fond, or not so fond, memories with her. Finally I'd like to thank Sue for coming up with such a wonderful idea and for her kindness with this great book in choosing to support CHAS.[*]

Children's Hospice Association Scotland
Sharing the Caring

* At Sue's request, the publisher, Headline Publishing Group Limited ('HPG') has donated £1000 from her advance and will donate 1% of the total royalty income to Children's Hospice Association Scotland (registered charity number: SC019724 – 'CHAS'). HPG will not be paid by CHAS in respect of these donations.

'What is patriotism but the love of
the food one ate as a child?'

Lin Yutang, 1895–1976

introduction

Sue Lawrence, food writer
born 1955

One of my earliest memories involving food was New Year. Because we lived in Edinburgh, we used to drive to Dundee on New Year's Day (having checked the ferry times over the River Forth – this was pre-Forth Road Bridge) and undertake a 'royal tour'. There were so many relatives to visit: for Dad to have his dram, Mum her sherry and my sister Carol and me our blackcurrant cordial. I remember in particular visiting Great Auntie Maggie at number 12 Baxter Park Terrace, in a tenement block just beside where my dad was brought up at number 10. Her flat was on the first floor and I remember being amazed that there was no bedroom, the bed being a part of the sitting room overlooking the park; the back room, overlooking the green, had the tiniest of sculleries off it, the size of a large cupboard.

I must have been about three when I first remember sipping cordial from a tiny glass and eating shortbread or sultana cake, both served with a wedge of cheese. The New Year visits would continue all day: I recall Auntie May in the 1960s having a 'Party Susan', serving cubes of cheese and pineapple, pickled onions and other nibbles; Granny Ward always bought delicious Toffee Cups especially for my sister and me. The day would end up at Granny Anderson's for steak pie and mashed potatoes and then the grand finale: cloutie dumpling with silver threepennies in it.

There is another Dundee scene ingrained on my memory which, rather improbably, unites Charles Dickens and Marcel Proust. It was teatime at Granny Anderson's house. Around the table were twinsetted aunts and freshly scrubbed cousins; tea was moving on apace – from steak pie to pudding – and with the ice cream, which Uncle Frank ran to the Italian ice-cream shop to buy (no freezers), were Tunnock's Snowballs.

I can still remember biting through the coconut-studded chocolate shell into the gloriously sticky, snow-white goo within. I can also remember the sudden silence that fell upon the erstwhile Hovis-like scene when I said loudly, mouth still full, 'Can I have another Snowball?' Not, 'Please may I have some more?', as Oliver Twist might have said, or merely retained a silent longing as Marcel Proust did for page upon page.

So, when my wonderful yet formidable granny asked me, from the other end of the table, to repeat my request, the entire family stared. My Pollyanna politeness had temporarily departed with my greedy desire for another Snowball and it was only when my cousin David whispered to me, 'You've forgotten to say "please",' that I was able to breathe and remember my manners.

Back in Eskbank, outside Edinburgh, where we lived, I remember being at school, in Primary 1 and so proud of my wonderful red shoes – until a wasp somehow got inside them and stung my foot. I cannot remember the pain, only being rushed off to the Staff Room and being allowed to sit and eat as many digestive biscuits as I wanted from a large McVitie's biscuit tin, until my mum came to collect me and take me home.

I also remember wasps buzzing around the garden near the kitchen window when my mum was making preserves every summer – raspberry jam or blackcurrant jelly. Then my sister and I would sit on the draining board on either side of the big kitchen sink to wash our feet after a summer's day barefoot in the garden, and eat the jam still warm on Scotch pancakes, fresh from the girdle (griddle).

Later on, at Scripture Union Camp on Arran, where my friend Isabelle and I went each year from the age of twelve, wasps featured heavily. Although most years were so wet we had to abandon the tents and sleep on tables in the dining tent at the top of the field, one year there was a heatwave. And so, at each al fresco meal, we had to lay out Wasp Bait: a slice of bread spread thickly with jam and placed in the middle of the table. The wasps would alight and we would whack them violently with a spoon. By the end of the meal there were piles of jammy corpses, which seemed somehow incongruous given the purpose of the camp.

At lunch at Senior School, there was never any choice of meal. If it was a liver and onions day and you loathed liver, then, tough – and it usually was! Still, on roast potato day the queues formed early outside the lunch hall and the minute we sat down we picked up our forks and plunged them greedily into the biggest, crispiest roast potato in the bowl in the middle of the table. As Grace was being said, we clung onto the end of our forks for dear life, until we were allowed to pile up our plates. There were also repulsive dishes such as the lumpiest custard with the thickest skin imaginable, and what we charmingly referred to as YMCA (Yesterday's Muck Cooked Again): this was trifle.

Between the ages of seven and about fourteen, I spent most of my life outside my own home at the manse, where Isabelle lived. Mrs Doig's meatloaf and her chocolate pudding were divine, and it was there I would have my first taste of such un-Scottish dishes as boiled rice with chicken – a legacy of their years spent in Africa. I was usually asked to stay for tea and always accepted, gobbling down as much as I could before politely thanking Mrs Doig and leaving, only to run up the road – a good half mile – to my own home where I never told my mum about the manse tea, but simply sat down to a second tea. It was at one of Isabelle's birthday parties that I recall challenging her big brother Peter to a food race. I remember sitting in the dining room with him, both of us eating more and more sandwiches and cakes and trifle until at last I surrendered; he beat me by one Ritz cracker!

Nowadays, when looking through my mum's old recipe jotters with scribbled scraps of paper and pages torn out of magazines, I become nostalgic. Titles that leap out at me are those recipes I loved. From Mum's jotters, her sultana cake, cheese pudding, 'macaroni AND cheese', treacle scones, guggy cake, Border tart, and one of her later treats: ginger torte. From school days there are torn-out pages, probably from arithmetic jotters, with 'Baked Macaroni' topped with potato crisps, 'Toffee Cake' involving two threepenny bars of Highland Toffee, and 'Triple Decker Squares' (the old name for millionaire's shortbread). There is a recipe scribbled by a school chum for 'Chewy Stuff' (marshmallows, toffee, margarine, Rice Krispies) which asks me at the end 'Do you have a recipe for coconut balls?' (Luckily, four decades on, I do; if only I knew who had wanted it!) I recognise my sister's neat handwriting for 'Cheese and Sardine Tricorns', Mrs Hamilton's recipe for chocolate fudge, and Mrs Marshall's coffee buns.

With just one look at these smudgy pages I am transported back to my childhood and recall not only the taste and sight of the recipe (usually sweet), but also the provenance. And that is the wonderful thing about asking people about their childhood food memories. At the interviews for this book, I have encountered sadness, deep nostalgia, even tears on recalling something a mum or granny used to make. I have also witnessed laughter, disdain and passion. But most of all I have seen an enthusiasm about the food my interviewees ate as children and teenagers. On the whole, it was home-cooked, fresh and seasonal: how could that not evoke a delicious nostalgia? I spent many months interviewing the prominent Scots in this book and am hugely grateful to them for their time – and their recipes! Most of the dishes appear as told to me by the interviewees but if they didn't have one to hand, I have suggested a recipe of my own.

Hopefully by trying some of these dishes and reading the accompanying tales, you too can recall your own childhood food memories and so forge that link to the past that Proust wrote about, but instead of Madeleines, think mince, broth or shortbread. Taste the memory...

Guggy Cake
makes 1 loaf

This delicious, moist cake is based on one from my mum's regular teatime repertoire. I still have her original recipe, torn from a magazine from 1963, which used only cups for measurements and lard instead of butter.

150g/5½ oz light muscovado sugar
150g/5½ oz sultanas
150g/5½ oz currants
125g/4½ oz butter

2 tsp mixed spice
225g/8 oz self-raising flour
pinch of salt
butter, for greasing

Place the first 5 ingredients in a heavy saucepan with 250ml/9 fl oz cold water. Heat gently until the butter is melted, then remove from the heat and cool.

Once cold, sift in the flour and a pinch of salt and combine well. Tip into a buttered, base-lined, 1kg/2 lb 4 oz loaf tin, levelling the surface, and bake in an oven preheated to 180ºC/350ºF/Gas 4 for about 1 hour or until a skewer inserted into the middle comes out clean. Remove to a wire rack to cool before turning out.

Serve sliced, spread with butter.

soups and
starters

Kirsty Young, broadcaster
born 1968

Kirsty Young's first food memory was connected to her being naughty: her mother had just put a dish of rice pudding onto the kitchen table to cool then gone away. 'I went up with a spoon and took two huge spoonfuls, then tried madly to cover up the indentations, flattening the top over so no-one would know I had taken any!' She still loves rice pudding to this day.

Kirsty's grandmothers were both good cooks. Her paternal granny, Jessie Young, was 'an unbelievable baker', making wonderful shortbread and tablet but also the best birthday cakes, topped with royal icing. She also made lots of jams and pale jellies, often using berries collected by Kirsty.

'My other grandmother, Annie Allan, was not a fancy cook, but she made good, simple food such as potato soup and fried fish. Her apple pie was also delicious – more what we would call *tarte aux pommes* nowadays, but without a lid! When my mum asked her for the recipe she tried it and it didn't work. It was probably because Granny had to make something from nothing – she had to feed five children and a husband on very little – and so when she said to Mum to use one large apple, she probably used all the bits we would throw in the bin too!'

Kirsty's favourite childhood dishes are many, but she particularly likes Scottish plain bread and potato scones. When she returns to Scotland her mum cooks her a proper breakfast with home-made potato scones and black pudding, which she loves. Kirsty remembers the thrill of going out to a restaurant for her sister's birthday when they were children and having gammon and pineapple – which at the time was very 'modern'. She also fondly recalls her mum's pineapple upside-down cake. At Christmas her granny would serve smoked salmon first, which Kirsty came to adore, even though this seemed to her a very unusual taste. Another strange taste she recalls vividly was the combination of mushy peas with vinegar and a milkshake – served at a seaside café in Millport. This was where the family used to go on holiday from East Kilbride (where Kirsty lived until she was seven), and then from Stirling, her subsequent home.

Kirsty remembers her mother's cooking being pretty healthy – nothing fried, only grilled – though they were allowed the occasional treat of a fish supper when on holiday. Her mum's lasagne, she thought, 'was simply sophistication beyond my wildest dreams; I still crave that and Mum makes it for me when I am home'.

And as for childhood dislikes: 'We were never allowed to be fussy, we just ate everything! Though I do remember the most revolting combination at school dinners of watery mashed potatoes with Spam and baked beans.'

Kirsty learned to cook when she was seventeen, while working as an au pair, but her love for all things to do with food had started much earlier. At thirteen she began cutting out food reviews from the papers, such as Loyd Grossman from *Harpers & Queen* magazine, and she bought her first cookery book in Glasgow when aged twenty. 'It was a perfect choice for my first cookbook, really – *An Omelette and a Glass of Wine*, by Elizabeth David!'

Nowadays Kirsty likes to cook Scottish dishes such as soups (Scotch broth like her mum's) or steak pie or haggis. 'But if I want to cook haggis at home, that has to be when my husband is out as he does not like it at all.'

Memories of her Granny Allan's cloutie dumpling make Kirsty very nostalgic: 'It was so delicious, it was almost beyond belief. And when First Footing at Hogmanay, I loved the shortbread – and I was allowed a snowball (Advocaat and lemonade) if I was really lucky!'

Lentil and Ham Hock Soup
serves 4–6

approx. 175g/6 oz red lentils
soup stock made from a ham hock
    (or another tasty stock will do – but
    you would need to add chopped bacon
    to it), reserving some flecks of meat
25g–55g/1–2 oz butter
3 carrots, peeled and chopped

1 onion (or 1 chopped leek), peeled
    and chopped
1 medium potato (if the stock is
    over-salty), peeled and chopped
a handful of fresh parsley leaves,
    chopped

Add the lentils to the stock in a large saucepan and cook until thoroughly tenderised.

In the meantime, melt the butter in another saucepan and gently sauté the carrots, onion (or leek) and potato (if required). Add all these vegetables to the ham and lentil stock and simmer until you have a delicious soup.

Add the chopped parsley and some flecks of meat from the ham hock, then serve with a nice stick of French bread. Some people liquidise this soup to a thick creamy consistency before serving, but I never do this as I much prefer the look and taste as it is.

Sandy Lyle, golfer
born 1958

Sandy Lyle remembers stovies with great fondness, but his first real food memory was of a bowl of lentil soup, and being allowed to eat the ham off the shank as a treat. This soup became one of his favourite dishes as a child, and indeed he still loves a good bowl of it now: 'Especially during the cold winter days when you just can't beat a nice warming bowl of soup.'

One dish he remembers loathing as a child was tripe, for both 'its disgusting smell and texture'. However, his mum was a good baker as her sisters had their own little bakery shop in Milngavie, just outside Glasgow, and so she always made sure the family could enjoy some home baking: scones, shortbread (millionaire's) or pancakes.

The family never ate out much, although as Sandy got older they might go out for a Chinese or an Indian meal. Of his early visits to golf courses he recalls, 'On special outings we would go to the hotel restaurant at the golf course, which we also did at Christmas time. I hated it, because I'd rather have stayed home to play with my presents!'

Nowadays, Sandy can get by with cooking and is good at grilling – anything from a steak to asparagus – on the barbecue. 'But as for cooking special dishes, I will have to leave that to my dear wife. We still enjoy a fair bit of home baking, made by our trusty right and left hand, Carol, who is from Dunbar and helps look after the children; she has the touch and the patience!'

As for cooking Scottish dishes himself at home, 'Well, if you can call it cooking, maybe sticking some haggis in the microwave – and boiling and mashing the veggies! In our household I am more known for the Full Monty breakfast, with any style of eggs from our own hens.'

On trips back to Scotland, Sandy loves to eat 'anything that is tasty! First port of call will be the curry house. And, for home cooking, I love to get anything out of the Aga that has been slowly cooked, with lots of flavour. The kids and I love a mean Thai and luckily Jolande, my wife, has that down to a fine art. The rice cooker is probably our most-used kitchen gadget.'

Spicy Lentil Soup

serves 6–8

This is an adaptation of my mum's original lentil soup. If you don't have lentils, just add some chickpeas or a couple of potatoes to thicken it a bit. If you spot some Dutch smoked sausage, cut it into little cubes and add it to your bowl, either at the table or just before serving. And don't forget the bread for dunking!

butter
2 onions, peeled and chopped
some crushed dried chillies
a few black peppercorns, whole
a little brown sugar, to taste

2–3 bay leaves
1 ham hock
a couple of handfuls of red lentils
3–4 carrots, peeled and chopped
salt and pepper

Start by making the stock. Brown the chopped onions in a little butter in a large, ovenproof casserole, add the crushed chillies, the peppercorns, brown sugar, bay leaves and the hock. Cover with water, bring to the boil and put the casserole into the simmering oven of the Aga (or about 150ºC/300ºF/Gas 2 in a normal oven).

Once you think you have a nice-smelling and tasty stock, take out the hock and bay leaves, discarding the bay leaves. Add the lentils and carrots and stick it back in the oven.

In the meantime, pull the ham off the bone, ready to go back into the soup. (I like to keep some aside as it tastes great on some home-made soda bread.)

When the lentils and carrots are soft, blend, season to taste, add the ham, and you are good to go.

Nicola Sturgeon,
Deputy First Minister of Scotland
born 1970

Growing up in Irvine, in North Ayrshire, Nicola Sturgeon's earliest childhood food memories were, like those of so many other Scots, of her mum's mince and potatoes. 'We ate out only very occasionally, my favourite restaurant was a sit-in fish and chip shop in Prestwick, where I had the classic fish supper.'

Her gran was a great cook, and Nicola loved her Sunday roast with Yorkshire puddings. She also fondly remembers steak pie on New Year's Day, again cooked by her gran. One dish she hated was liver: 'I didn't like the taste of liver or even the thought of it!'

Nowadays there are certain childhood dishes that she still craves: 'I love sausages and mash, a great favourite from when I was small; you can't beat it for comfort food!' Nicola admits to being a terrible cook, but says she can turn her hand to soup – 'Vegetable soup is my only speciality' – and lentil soup is one of her regular dishes.

Bacon, Lentil and Kale Soup
serves 6

Sue says: This is my soup, made especially for Nicola. I like a sprinkling of grated Mull Cheddar on top too.

1 tbsp olive oil
5–6 rashers smoked streaky bacon,
   chopped
2 carrots, peeled and chopped
4 sticks celery, chopped
1 onion, peeled and chopped
150g/5½ oz dried green lentils
   (the no-soak variety)

225g can chopped tomatoes
1.7 litres/3 pints ham stock
150g/5½ oz washed and shredded
   kale (this is the prepared weight)
salt and pepper, to taste

Heat the oil in a large pan and sauté the bacon for a few minutes. Add the carrots, celery and onion. Continue to sauté for a few minutes.

Wash and drain the lentils then add to the pan with the tomatoes and stock. Bring to the boil then simmer for about 35–40 minutes. Add the kale and continue to cook for a further 10–15 minutes or until the kale is tender. Add some boiling water if it is too thick. Season to taste with salt and pepper before serving.

Scotch Broth

serves 6

The beef is cooked to flavour the stock, then it should be removed before serving.

350g/12 oz piece marrow bone
1.4kg/3 lb 2 oz piece beef skirt
300ml/10 fl oz broth mix
2 medium carrots, peeled and finely
    chopped
2 medium onions, peeled and finely
    chopped

1 medium parsnip, finely chopped
¼ white cabbage, finely chopped
1 leek, finely chopped
1–2 level tbsp salt
2 level tbsp freshly chopped parsley,
    to serve

Put the marrow bone and beef skirt into a large saucepan and add 2.6 litres/4½ pints cold water (or enough to cover the meat). Bring to the boil, remove any scum and discard. Turn the heat down low, add the broth mix and simmer, partly covered, for 1½ hours, skimming the surface occasionally.

Add the carrots, onions, parsnip, cabbage and leek and another 600ml/1 pint water to the pan, cover to bring to the boil quickly, then simmer for another 30 minutes.

Remove the bone and beef from the soup. Season with salt and pepper, stir in the chopped parsley, and serve.

David Coulthard,
Formula One racing driver
born 1971

David Coulthard's earliest childhood food memory was one that is familiar to so many of us: 'It was ice cream and jellies at parties.'

Food was important when he was growing up in Kirkcudbrightshire in the 1970s. His mum was always cooking and made fantastic soup; indeed, his favourite childhood dishes are still his mum's soups. Another great memory was of a full Scottish breakfast on a Sunday.

As a family, eating out was not a regular pastime, as there was not much choice of restaurants in rural Scotland; but they did go out for bar snacks.

David hated vegetables: 'Because my mother steamed them (the healthy option, I now realise), they were very hard. Today, though, I love them.' Now when David returns to Scotland he loves to eat 'anything fresh'.

Tattie Soup
serves 4

Sue says: This is my tattie soup recipe, one of David's favourites.

1.2 litres/2 pints good chicken stock
1kg/2 lb 4 oz potatoes, peeled
1 large onion, peeled

3–4 carrots, peeled
salt and pepper, to taste
chopped fresh chives or parsley
    leaves, to garnish

Bring the stock to the boil in a large saucepan.

Chop the vegetables into similarly sized dice and add to the pan, along with some salt and pepper. Cover and cook over a medium heat for 25–30 minutes until the vegetables are all tender. Taste and check the seasoning.

Ladle the soup into bowls and sprinkle each bowl with some chives or parsley.

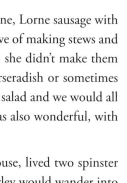

Shirley Spear, chef
born 1952

One of Shirley Spear's first memories is of sitting in a pram seat, her brother in the pram and being taken to the clinic for tins of baby milk and bottles of orange juice with a blue cap. She also recalls being given a tablespoon of malt from a big brown jar and a daily dose of rosehip syrup. Shirley told me how she collected rosehips when she was at primary school and was given six pence a pound for them (presumably to make the syrup). I too recall this early form of child labour!

Food was important in Shirley's house when she was growing up, but since there were five children it was always good but simple fare. Shirley remembers helping her mum roll out pastry for jam tarts and her mum insisting on putting her – by now grey – pastry cases on the garden fence for the birds to eat instead of the family! There was always lots of home baking going on when she lived in Peebles (where they lived until she was eight, before they moved to Edinburgh), as people were always popping in for a cup of tea. There would be shortbread, fairy cakes, Victoria sponge, and for special occasions or parties they would make 'chocolate truffles' from porridge oats, coconut and cocoa mixed with melted margarine and syrup, formed into balls then rolled in coconut. 'Mum's meringues were also really good, nicely gooey in the middle. We would fill them with tinned Nestlé cream.'

Daily meals would consist of mince, liver and onions, fish in Ruskoline, Lorne sausage with fried egg and slow-cooked stews. 'I've inherited from my mum the love of making stews and casseroles,' says Shirley, 'and though I also adore making soups now, she didn't make them often. We would always have a family Sunday roast – beef with horseradish or sometimes mutton, always with roast potatoes. And there was often tinned fruit salad and we would all end up arguing over the cherry from the tin! Mum's rice pudding was also wonderful, with a lovely, brown, nutmeggy skin.'

At the end of their road in Peebles, a few doors down from their house, lived two spinster sisters and their brother, who was a shepherd. Sometimes young Shirley would wander into their house around lunchtime as she was fascinated by the daily ritual: the brother would arrive home from the farm, sit on the stairs to remove his boots, then at the table his sisters would serve him an entire shepherd's pie in an oblong enamel tin. 'He would eat the lot! And of course I thought – for many years in fact – that the pie was so-called because he was a shepherd! He always had Pan Drops in his pocket and I would always come home with some – much to Mum's horror, as she was concerned about the proximity of sweeties to dirty handkerchiefs!'

Hallowe'en is a festival that Shirley feels strongly about: 'I feel very sad about Hallowe'en, as it has been hijacked by the Americans, though in Scotland we have always celebrated it. I remember having to howk out a turnip, then use string for the handles and pop a candle inside. The smell of the burnt raw turnip is an abiding memory. We often had Hallowe'en parties at home and we would make papier mâché witches as decoration and I would help Mum make toffee apples. There would be tablet and treacle scones and we would dook for apples. I remember once going guysing dressed as one of three highwaymen with my two chums. We had my brother's cowboy gun with us and I had bought some penny caps to fire, and we ended our song and dance routine at the doors with a shot of the gun and a cry of "Your money or your life", which horrified my mother as we were not allowed to ask for money, as the kids nowadays seem to expect. One of my favourite ways of using the insides of a turnip after hours of turnip lantern-making, is in soup.'

Neep Bree

serves 6

Bree is an old Scottish word for a broth. This is a great lunchtime soup and perfect with some warm cheese scones, straight from the oven, on a cold day.

50g/1¾ oz butter

2 medium or large onions, peeled and
    chopped small

1 large neep (a yellow, swede turnip),
    peeled and diced small (weighing
    approx. 500g/1 lb 2 oz when
    prepared)

piece of whole root ginger, approx.
    the size of the top of your thumb,
    finely grated

salt and pepper, to taste

juice and finely grated rind of
    1 large orange

1 litre/1¾ pints vegetable stock

approx. 125ml/4 fl oz milk

125ml/4 fl oz double cream,
    to serve

finely chopped fresh chives,
    to garnish

Melt the butter in a large saucepan until foaming. Add the onions and cook until soft, but not brown. Stir in the turnip and mix well. Add the grated ginger, plus some salt and freshly ground black pepper. Put the lid on and allow the vegetables to cook gently for 5–10 minutes, stirring occasionally.

Pour in the orange juice and rind. Stir well. Add the stock, bring to boil and then reduce the heat and simmer slowly, with the lid on, for 1 hour.

Add the milk and liquidise thoroughly. (The soup can be cooled and frozen at this stage.) Check the seasoning to taste and stir the cream through. Heat thoroughly before serving. (If too thick, add a little more milk or cream, especially if reheating from cold.)

Serve with a sprinkling of finely chopped chives and some warm cheese scones.

Wholemeal Cheese Scones
makes 12

When we first opened The Three Chimneys on Skye, I served these scones with home-made soup at lunchtimes. We still have customers who remember driving all the way to us to enjoy a bowl of neep bree with warm cheese scones – especially on a cold, Skye day! They are best served soon after they are baked, but they also freeze well.

100g/3½ oz wholemeal self-raising flour
100g/3½ oz white self-raising flour
½ tsp table salt
½ tsp mustard powder
¼ tsp cayenne pepper
1 scant level tsp bicarbonate of soda

40g/1½ oz Scottish butter, diced
200g/7 oz mature white Scottish
   Cheddar cheese, finely grated
1 large free-range egg
approx. 75–100ml/2½–3½ fl oz
   fresh milk

Sift the flours together with the salt, mustard powder, cayenne and bicarbonate of soda. Rub in the butter to the dry ingredients, using the tips of your fingers. Add the grated cheese and mix together lightly with your fingers.

Beat the egg and 75ml/2½ fl oz of the milk together, add to the mixture and bind to make a smooth dough, using the rounded blade of a table knife. Add more milk if necessary.

Using your hands, gently pull the dough together in the mixing bowl to form a smooth ball, adding a little more milk if the mixture seems too dry. Place the dough on a floured board and roll it out evenly to a thickness of 4cm/1½ in – no thinner. Cut out the scones with a 5cm/2 in straight-sided cutter, pushing down into the dough without twisting it. This helps to make the scones rise evenly.

Place the scones on a floured baking tray and lightly brush the tops of each with a little more milk. Finally, sprinkle the remaining grated cheese on the top of each scone.

Bake on the centre shelf of an oven preheated to 220ºC/425ºF/Gas 7, for 12–15 minutes or until risen and golden.

Remove to a cooling tray. Resist eating until you are ready to serve!

Alex Salmond,
Scotland's First Minister
born 1954

Alex Salmond remembers 'winding' molten tablet round a wooden spoon in the kitchen of his Linlithgow home as a toddler. He also recalls, when he was slightly older, being allowed to stir the bubbling mass in the pan. Made from Carnation milk because of his severe allergy to cow's milk (for some reason Carnation milk was acceptable), he smiled at the memory of his mother's tablet: 'No-one makes it like that now.'

His was a house of all-home cooking, without any convenience foods. His mum was an excellent cook and baker, as was his grandmother. His aunt worked in Oliphant's, the baker's in Linlithgow, and so had no need to bake at home. This was the shop where, Alex told me, 'they made the best muffins in Scotland. The queues every Saturday went on for ever.'

But it was his mother's Christmas cakes that were the talk of the town. 'She would make some fifty each year, to give out to extended family, friends and "old folk". I used to dispatch them. My Great Auntie Aggie's birthday was New Year's Day and I remember going to her house with her cake in particular. My birthday is on Hogmanay, and so in our family we had two days of ongoing celebrations!' Alex describes his mother's cakes very fondly: 'These were serious cakes. I remember the packets of dried fruit all over the kitchen and then, once they were all done – some were iced, some left for the recipient to ice – they were foil-wrapped before being sent out. They lasted for ages. Indeed, though my mother died in 2003, we kept one of her cakes and still enjoyed it, albeit with a slight hint of sadness and nostalgia, three or four years later.'

As well as the myriad cakes he had to help distribute, Alex's mother's Christmas puddings were also legendary, but these were made only for the immediate family. They used to ignite them with brandy on Christmas Day and he vividly recalls the flames: 'On more than one occasion, they seemed to set everything alight, not just the pudding!'

One of Alex's favourite childhood dishes was rice pudding, which he adored – skin and all. Of course, it was not made with cow's milk but with goat's milk, on which he practically lived. Fortunately, there were goats nearby and their milk was specially delivered to the Salmond house. He also remembers wonderful picnics, perhaps into the Bathgate Hills and, in particular, the squashed tomato sandwiches: 'The bread got all squashed from the soft tomatoes – and the foil they were wrapped in somehow gave them a better taste!'

Sunday school picnics were also a huge treat, but he has never forgotten the traumatic picnic of 1963 when, all of eight years old, he didn't get his Lucky Bag. The teachers had simply forgotten to give him the special bag containing an apple, a bag of crisps, chocolate biscuit and a bar of McGowan's Highland toffee. His wistful look suggested to me that he still feels peeved that he was the only child not to receive the Lucky Bag all those years ago!

While growing up, Alex learned to cook very little – apart from that wonderful tablet – but at university he mastered most student dishes, such as spaghetti Bolognese, and sometimes he would even save up to buy steak, as it was so easy to cook. There was no food he loathed, apart from tinned spaghetti.

Alex took part in a recent campaign to promote Scottish food by eating only Scottish produce for a week, and he survived admirably. He shopped for everything himself and cooked it all; each meal costing no more than £1 a head.

Another Scottish dish Alex adores is steak pie ('My wife Moira makes a serious steak pie!'), but he also loves good Scottish butchers' pies, citing butchers in Aberdeen, Inverurie and Huntly as some of the best. His mother used to make steak pie for New Year's Day (followed by cloutie dumpling or trifle), but also for The Marches. This is a centuries-old tradition that takes place in Linlithgow on the first Tuesday after the second Thursday in June. In the town it is still a very important event, and so steak pie, just as at New Year, was part of the celebration.

Cullen Skink

serves 4

Sue says: Alex's wife Moira got this recipe from the chef at the Pennan Inn on the Banffshire coast, but the word 'skink' brings back other memories for Alex, as his dad used to call him a skink as a child because he was so skinny!

2 medium smoked haddock fillets or
   1 large finnan haddock
2 medium onions, peeled and chopped
55g/2 oz butter, plus a knob for the mash

450g/1 lb potatoes, peeled
425ml/¾ pint milk
salt and pepper, to taste
chopped fresh parsley, to garnish

Place the fish in a pan with enough cold water to cover. Bring slowly to the boil and simmer for 10 minutes. Take out the fish, retaining the liquor, then remove and discard the bones and skin. Flake the fish.

In another pan, cook the onions in the butter.

Boil the potatoes in another pan, and when cooked, mash them with the knob of butter before adding the liquor from the fish, the milk and onion (and buttery juices). Add salt and pepper to taste, then serve in warm bowls with parsley scattered on top.

Chicken Soup with Rice

serves 6

Chicken soup was Sunday fare, usually with a couple of slices of plain bread (from the cheapest wax-wrapped packet) for dipping, to bulk us up. Leftover chicken followed on Monday. I still make this.

For the stock:

1 whole, medium-sized, free-range
    chicken from a butcher
1 large onion, split in two
2–3 large, whole carrots
a couple of stalks of celery, whole

salt and pepper, to taste
bay leaves
some parsley stalks
    (retain the leaves for the soup)

Put the chicken (with the skin on, or it will fall to bits) in a big pot with the onion, carrots, celery, seasoning and herbs (plus whatever other little bits of flavouring you fancy). Barely cover the bird with water and bring to the boil. Once it's rolling, reduce the heat to a simmer and let it cook for around an hour and a half or until it looks as though the flesh is ready to fall away from the bones. Take it off the heat and remove the chicken right away. Let the water (now stock) cool, then sieve it to take out the veg and whatever fat has accumulated on top. Now you can use it to make lovely soup.

For the soup:

the cooked chicken
1 stick celery, chopped small
2–3 leeks, finely chopped
2 bay leaves
a knob of butter
salt and pepper, to taste

the stock
175g/6 oz/1 cup long-grain rice,
    washed under the tap
a big handful of chopped fresh parsley
a few chopped greentails (spring onions)

Shred all the chicken meat off the carcass and set aside.

In a large pot, add the celery, leeks and bay leaves to the butter and fry very lightly until they soften but do not brown (only a few minutes). Season this vegetable mixture with salt and pepper.

Pour in the sieved or skimmed stock (you might prefer to use only half or three-quarters of it if you want less soup) and gently bring it to the boil. Add the rice and simmer the whole lot for around 20 minutes at most.

Stir in as much shredded chicken as you fancy and season again to taste. Add the chopped parsley and greentails last, and serve with sliced bread and a lump of Ayrshire Dunlop cheese on the side.

veg, cheese and breakfast

BREAD

Bill Paterson, actor
born 1945

'I have a terrible memory of an egg – it might have been fried or boiled, but it was ghastly. I could only have been a toddler as I remember sitting in a wooden high chair. Ever since then I have never been able to be in the same building as a fried or boiled egg!' Bill Paterson's first childhood food memories are not good, but he has overcome some of his egg prejudices: 'From about the age of twenty I was able to eat an omelette or scrambled eggs, but never a fried or boiled egg!'

As Bill Paterson was growing up in his Dennistoun tenement in Glasgow, there was good food at home, his mum being 'a spectacular soup- and jam-maker'. She made chicken soup, lentil soup and Scotch broth. Every summer she made jams from fruits in season; blackcurrant, raspberry and strawberry jams were made from shop-bought fruit, but she would also make bramble jam from the berries Bill and his friends would pick for her. 'I remember the press in the front room always being well stocked: the entire bottom shelves were laden with jars of neatly labelled jam.'

His granny, who was from Lochaber, made tattie scones on her old-fashioned girdle, or griddle (the type made to hang over a fire). Bill also vividly remembers his Highland granny's favourite snack of oatcakes with Gorgonzola cheese, which must have been a bit of a rarity in 1940s Scotland!

His Auntie Polly, who ran a guest house in Dunoon, made wonderful ham and lentil soup, one of his favourite childhood dishes, along with cheese on toast, which he would make with his dad: they would spear bread and toast it in front of the fire then put the cheese on top (good Scottish Cheddar) and finish it off under the grill.

As well as eggs, Bill also hated milk puddings such as tapioca and rice puddings; custard, though, he liked – particularly when his mum stirred in some cocoa powder to make chocolate custard. He also loathed tripe and potted hough, the latter for its gelatinous texture.

He admits he was a faddy child and didn't enjoy eating at anyone else's house. If he was playing at a friend's house and was invited to stay for tea, he would make some excuse to get home. Bill's dad was a commercial traveller and would often eat out in hotels, and if Bill went with him, what might otherwise seem a luxury for a child was for him torture. He would always have the breaded fish, which he felt was safe.

Fish and chips, however, were a treat: they lived above a Scots–Italian café called the Swallow Café, whose fish and chips were very good. For one shilling and ten pence (about nine pence in new money) he could buy a delicious fish supper. Since, as well as the chip shop, there was also a butcher's shop beneath their tenement block, they would have steak pie, 'an asset pie, delicious stewed beef underneath a crust and placed in the characteristic metallic dish, which we would return empty to the butcher, ready to be filled with our next steak pie.'

As a teenager, since he never took school dinners, Bill came home for lunch and used to make himself something with ham and tomato, and usually some chips. His mum would have peeled and cut the potatoes and left them in a bowl of cold water so that all he had to do was deep-fry them. Even though he was about fourteen, Bill reckons no working mum would even consider allowing a young son home alone these days to 'play' with boiling fat!

Nowadays he loves to cook herring in oatmeal, if he can find herring fillets. And he loves shortbread and tablet but finds it difficult not to finish the entire packet. Bill remembers going to church sales of work: 'The purpose of them for us was purely to get tablet. We used to go there only to get Mrs Cameron's or Mrs McFadgeon's tablet.'

Whenever he returns to Scotland from London, Bill loves eating kippers for breakfast: 'It's always good to eat them in a hotel as, easy though they are to do at home, the smell lingers and I get a row!' He also loves Lorne (square) sausage, which, when he is filming in Scotland, is the film crew's favourite, although, he says, 'Lorne sausage is wonderful, but only eat it if you can square it first with your cardiologist!'

But another favourite is tattie scones, which is how Bill uses leftover mashed potato, as he always makes far too much. 'For multi-cultural Scots, it also works with a combination of sweet potatoes and regular ones. The girdle [griddle] from my granny is a family heirloom and virtually indestructible.' The scones are also good with houmous or tapenade, 'for that fusion experience unheard of in my granny's Lochaber!'

Tattie Scones
makes 8

Sue says: This is my own scone recipe especially for Bill.

1 large potato (about 250g/9 oz)
25g/1 oz unsalted butter, plus
   extra for frying and serving

50g/2 oz plain flour
½ tsp salt
¼ tsp baking powder

Peel the potato, cut into chunks and cook in a pan of boiling water until tender, then drain well. Using a potato masher, mash the potato with the butter. Now weigh it: you need about 200g/7 oz mash.

Sift the flour, salt and baking powder into a bowl. While the mash is still warm, stir into the flour and combine well. Using lightly floured hands, gently shape this mixture into 2 balls and turn out onto a lightly floured surface. With a rolling pin, roll out gently to form 2 circles about 5mm/¼ in thick. Cut each circle into quarters. Prick all over with a fork.

Heat the girdle, or griddle (or heavy frying pan) to medium-hot, smear over a little butter then, once hot, transfer 4 scones to it with a large spatula or fish slice. Cook for about 3–4 minutes each side until golden brown. Transfer to a wire rack to cool briefly before spreading with a little butter and eating warm.

They can also be made in advance; loosely wrap them in foil and reheat them in a low oven when needed.

Viv Lumsden, broadcaster
born 1952

Viv Lumsden's first memories of food involve soup. 'There was always a pot of soup on the go – some dead beasties' bones would be boiling away in the kitchen every single day. It was mainly Scotch broth, and that is the one soup I never make now as I never liked the barley in it.'

Growing up in Edinburgh, Viv enjoyed good food at home. Although her mother was a 'modern working mother', and so more into quick food such as mince and tatties and beans on toast, her grandmother was a very good home cook. 'I called my grandmother (my mum's mum) Dan – and she was an angel, looked just like Maw Broon, very stout with a little bun on her head! She did great soups.'

Viv also used to love her grandmother's meatloaf, made with minced steak, minced ham and sausagemeat (bound with breadcrumbs and an egg). But this versatile mixture was also used as a casing for her grandmother's Scotch eggs, which she used to enjoy. Sometimes her grandmother would cook a whole ox tongue: 'It used to boil away for hours, all curled up in an enormous pan.' Another childhood favourite, albeit a rather unhealthy one, was salad cream sandwiches; beans on toast was also an almost daily staple.

Since her own family were not pudding people, Viv remembers really well her grandmother's cheese soufflé and her steamed puds, 'with the greaseproof paper and string tied intricately round the top then made into a handle. There was syrup and raisin, cloutie dumpling or apple sponge – there was always some spongey thing going on.' And Viv mentions that, although they would have three courses at least once a day, portions were so much smaller than now and, although it was perhaps not as varied as these days, their diet was balanced – and always reflected what was in season.

Viv's family never ate out when she was a child, but if they were on holiday and ate in the restaurant of the hotel, her father, 'whose taste was very narrow', would opt for a plain omelette (cheese omelette if he was feeling daring), or steak on special occasions. She recalls on rare trips going to Jenners for afternoon tea: one of her mother's friends was a model who used to go round the tables posing during tea, displaying the store's clothes to the ladies as they supped from their porcelain cups.

Viv has always loved potatoes: 'It's my home vegetable. I love potatoes of all description and never enjoyed plain boiled rice. One other thing I disliked as a child – apart from barley – was fish with bones. My mum would go to Musselburgh especially to buy her smokies or kippers, and as she arrived home drooling in anticipation of the fish, I was dreading the bones.'

Viv seems to find herself returning more and more now to the old Scots dishes such as mince, skirlie and soups. Another soup she remembered her other grandmother making was butter bean and Savoy cabbage, which she loathed as butter beans were – and still are – one of her top most hated foods. Turnip remains one of her favourite vegetables, though, and she remembers fondly the particular smell of the burnt lid on the turnip lantern that all Scottish children used to take round when guysing at Hallowe'en, having spent hours howking out the impenetrable insides of the neep. Happy days...

Cheese Soufflé
serves 2–3

Not really a soufflé, more of a baked cheese pudding, but a great favourite; this is one of my grandmother's recipes.

300ml/10 fl oz/1½ cups milk
55g/2 oz/1 cup fresh breadcrumbs
15g/½ oz butter
1 large egg, beaten

55g/2 oz grated cheese
½ tsp mustard (dried)
salt and pepper, to taste

Heat the milk until it reaches boiling point, then remove from the heat and add the breadcrumbs and butter.

Mix well with a fork or wooden spoon. Add the remaining ingredients, pour into an oven dish and bake in an oven preheated to 180°C/350°F/Gas 4 for about half an hour until just set.

Alex McLeish, footballer
born 1959

Alex's first memories of eating involve Farley's rusks; and these are very fond memories as he adored them well into his teens when, instead of having them soaked in hot milk, he would dunk them into his tea.

But what he also recalls from his childhood is the weekly routine of meals, which meant that Tuesday was always Mince Day. He was never a lover of mince; he used to hate the fatty bits and would pick out any greasy blobs. Now he adores steak mince without fat. Another night was The Fry Up, which would involve bacon, egg, tattie scone and, of course, a 'butcher's slice' – also known as square sausage or Lorne sausage, a square beef sausage. Another routine was Saturday morning, football day, when he would go to collect the papers and pick up the morning rolls: well-fired Glasgow rolls. These would be eaten with either bacon or a 'square slice'. Alex still enjoys these: 'When you develop a taste for these foods as a child, it never changes; I love them!'

Although he sometimes had to have school dinners during his Glasgow childhood (he lived in the East End, then Kinning Park, then moved to Barrhead when he was five), he also liked coming home at lunchtime. One of the things he would love for a home lunch was Smash (packet mashed potatoes) mixed with grated cheese. When I asked him about it, he told me, 'It's got to be packet. And though my tastes have – thankfully – evolved since, I still love it as a treat!'

Another childhood treat was toasted cheese at night; and egg in a cup, especially when he was ill in bed. This was an 'almost hard-boiled' egg (he did not like them runny), mashed with butter and salt and eaten in a cup with a spoon. His wife sometimes makes that for him these days, though he proudly says that is one of the few things he actually cooks himself at home.

The family never ate out, but on Friday night, when his dad got his wages slip, they would sometimes have fish and chips from the chip shop. When he was about thirteen or fourteen, he began to make good progress in both his school football team and the local football club, and his dad started insisting on buying him a chicken breast for tea on a Friday night to 'build him up' for Saturday's game. And so began the demise of the greasy Friday-night fish supper!

There was little he did not like to eat as a child. If he had a couple of shillings spare, he loved to buy a big cream meringue or a fresh cream strawberry tart from the baker's. His all-time favourite was a Paris bun with crunchy sugar on top. He also loved stovies, usually served just as it came, but when he moved to Aberdeen in 1976 he often had it with corned beef.

'Although my mother made fantastic soups, I hated lentil soup; I really didn't like the texture. But her greatest dish was steak and kidney pie, baked in an ashet [enamel pie dish] and served with beef link sausages. My granny made steak pie, too, and I have an early memory of sitting on my grandad's lap as he was eating straight from the ashet. I remember him feeding me bits of pastry and gravy from the wonderful pie made by Granny.'

Steak pie was the New Year's Day meal, always served with link sausages and often with kidneys in it too. This was usually served with boiled potatoes, but young Alex liked to re-invent his Smash dish by removing the skins from the boiled potatoes and mashing the insides down with lots of butter.

One of Alex's favourite dishes was macaroni cheese, which was a family regular. When I asked what it was served with, he said 'Well, certainly never with salad. It was served just by itself!'

Macaroni Cheese
serves 4

Sue says: Although Alex would disapprove, my dish is delicious served with roasted cherry tomatoes or a simple tomato salad and some crusty bread.

250g packet of Marshalls' macaroni
45g/1½ oz butter
50g/1¾ oz flour
500ml/16 fl oz whole milk

175g/6 oz grated Cheddar
salt and pepper, to taste
a handful each of fresh breadcrumbs
  and grated Cheddar, for topping

Boil the macaroni according to the packet instructions, then drain.

Meanwhile, melt the butter in a large saucepan, add the flour and, stirring well, cook for 2–3 minutes. Gradually whisk in the milk and simmer gently, whisking, for 10 minutes, then add the cheese and season to taste.

Stir the macaroni into the sauce, then tip it all into a shallow baking dish. Top with the breadcrumbs and extra cheese. Bake in an oven preheated to 180°C/350°F/Gas 4 for about 30 minutes.

Sir David Steel, politician, 1st Presiding Officer of the Scottish Parliament
born 1938

Sir David Steel was born in Kirkcaldy but brought up in both Kenya and Scotland, so his childhood memories also include less typically Scottish dishes such as home-made ice cream and fools made from tropical fruit.

His earliest memory, however, is even more unusual: 'I remember having to eat the rabbits kept in an outhouse during wartime rationing; this, however, was better than having to wear the smelly mittens made from their inadequately cured skins!'

One dish from his childhood that David still craves is good old mince and tatties; indeed, he asks, 'Why on earth can one never get that in restaurants in Scotland?'

A dish he loathed as a child growing up during the war was toad-in-the-hole, as it was made from wartime sausages and powdered egg. But he fondly recalls his mother's glorious dish of tripe and onions served with mashed potatoes – which she refused to eat herself!

One of David's favourite Scottish dishes nowadays is a good haggis with bashed neeps and champit tatties, but the one that reminds him most of his childhood is Welsh rarebit, which I have renamed Scottish rarebit for this book.

Scottish Rarebit
serves 1

Sue says: Here is my own rarebit recipe for David.

75g/2¾ oz Scottish farmhouse
    Cheddar, grated
1 tsp flour
2 tbsp milk
2 thick slices of bread
    (preferably wholemeal)

1 tsp Dijon mustard
1 tsp Worcestershire sauce
cayenne pepper, to taste

Put the cheese in a saucepan with the flour and milk and heat gently, stirring well, and put the bread on to toast. Once the cheese has melted, add the mustard and Worcestershire sauce. As soon as the mixture is smooth, pour it over the toast and shake over some pepper. Pop under a hot grill until golden.

Kirsty Wark, broadcaster
born 1955

Because her mother's family were the first commercial tomato growers on the Clyde, Kirsty Wark recalls halcyon days as a little girl, being surrounded by tomato plants. She vividly remembers being with her mother and aunt during the one day a year that was devoted to bottling. She came to understand the concept of 'home-made' very early on.

She also came to appreciate food in a rather un-Scottish way: by actually talking about its taste and feel and smell! As a child she was aware of the texture and aroma of the tomatoes, as she would be invited to touch and smell them. She also fondly remembers the fabulous taste of freshly made strawberry jam on white bread with butter.

Her mother always had a pot of soup on the go, and so too now does Kirsty. She sees cooking as very much a family thing – her son and husband cook, her daughter bakes and Kirsty does both. Even now she will make beef tea if someone is unwell, as that was the invalid food served when she was growing up: beef tied tightly in a pot with wax paper and string and boiled, then strained before being supped in bed.

But as for day-to-day meals, Kirsty reveals, 'there was always a routine when I was a child: a roast on Sundays, perhaps cauliflower cheese one night, then liver or haddock (smoked or fresh) on other nights of the week. And as a treat, a Green's crème caramel!' But there was very little that was not home-made, and Kirsty's mother's cake tins were always full. Favourites included tea bread (the loaf mixture soaked in tea overnight) and shortbread (her mother's was the best, with just a touch of cornflour to add a melt-in-the-mouth texture).

Kirsty enjoyed cooking as a child, and as well as the usual Scottish fare, she also remembers such exotic ingredients as melons being in the kitchen. These were such a treat: her mother would remove the seeds and place them in the oven to dry, then make necklaces with them! She also recalls dipping rhubarb into white sugar at her paternal grandmother's house, but since Kirsty lived in Kilmarnock, the first area in Scotland to have fluoride in the water, her teeth are not quite as full of fillings as most other 1950s rhubarb-dipping Scots children!

Kirsty seldom follows a recipe, but when she looks at her mother's old ones, perhaps smattered with butter, she says, 'I see these old recipes as a very tangible way of connecting with the past.'

Tomato Sauce

serves 4

I like serving this delicious sauce with pasta.

900g/2 lb halved and seeded tomatoes (skin on)
sea salt and black pepper, to sprinkle
olive oil, for drizzling and cooking
1 tsp sugar

3 cloves garlic, peeled and finely chopped
2 leeks, white part finely chopped
1 red onion, peeled and finely chopped

Liberally sprinkle the tomatoes with sea salt and black pepper and drizzle with olive oil. Roast in an oven preheated to 180°C/350°F/Gas 4 for 30 minutes.

Heat a little more olive oil with the sugar and sauté the garlic, leeks and onion until softened. Purée together with the tomatoes and serve with any type of cooked pasta.

Midge Ure, musician
born 1953

Midge Ure's earliest memory of food was mince, potatoes and butter beans – 'classic Scottish fare'. He remembers food being important, as he grew up in a tenement in Glasgow in the 1950s. Midge's dad was a van driver for a bakery, so he used to come home with tea cakes, morning rolls and crusty loaves, and his dad's father was a butcher, so he remembers having good sausages and stewing steak whenever his grandfather visited.

'We were never really into puddings. Besides, as there wasn't a table in the house until I was ten, we just ate on our laps so there was little time for two courses. We then moved out of the tenement into a modern council house with a bit more space for a table. But I do remember Creamola custard and some steamed puddings, especially a Heinz steamed syrup pudding in a tin that you had to pierce before boiling in a pan.

'One of my favourite dishes was stovies, but then I love peasant food throughout the world, whether it's pulses, potatoes or noodles. Stovies is our equivalent, a dish simply made of potatoes, onions and dripping. My granny made another of my favourites, which she called "Hot Chow". It was a stew made from potatoes, sausages and baked beans and was a derivation of stovies; quite weird, but delicious!'

Midge enjoyed fish suppers as a child and remembers that in Scottish chip shops all that was on offer was haddock, either battered or breadcrumbed. When he was older he used to try such treats as deep-fried black pudding or sausages, too.

There was only one thing he loathed as a child and that was offal. 'My dad used to eat lots of offal, such as liver and kidneys; he also ate tripe which I thought was so horrible as it looked just like a baby's nappy! If I even see a steak pie that has kidneys in it, I can't go near it.'

When Midge returns to Scotland he loves to go back to the places of his childhood and eat things he enjoyed then, such as a good Scotch pie from the butcher's or Lorne sausage with a fried egg and fried potato scone.

New Year was the only time that Midge's family ate anything that was traditional: 'We ate dinner at 10pm on Hogmanay; it was always an unusually late meal and it was always steak pie, which Mum used to make.' The pie was served with mashed potatoes and peas.

Nowadays he doesn't cook much in the way of Scottish dishes, as his one attempt at recreating the wonderful cloutie dumpling that was always made on birthdays was not entirely successful. 'I was so ham-fisted with it. But a dumpling to me is classic *Oor Wullie* stuff, with the ceremony of unwrapping the cloth and all.'

One of the dishes he does cook a lot these days is Blue Cheese Pasta, using a recipe given to him by his friend Mick Karm, bassist from the band Japan, who taught Midge to cook this simple but delicious dish.

Blue Cheese Pasta
serves 3–4

150g/5½ oz Stilton, crumbled
1 small tub Greek yoghurt
50g/1¾ oz pine nuts

300g/10 oz penne pasta
freshly ground black pepper, to taste

Melt the cheese very, very slowly in a pan until molten (do not overheat). Allow to cool until warm then slowly stir in the yoghurt until creamy.

Meanwhile, lightly toast the pine nuts in a hot pan until golden and tip into the sauce.

Cook the pasta according to the packet instructions then drain and tip into the sauce, tossing together with plenty of freshly ground black pepper. Serve warm.

Alan Cumming, actor

born 1965

Alan Cumming's earliest food memory is 'having mashed tattie sandwiches whilst pedalling round the kitchen in Fassfearn, near Fort William. They are an overlooked delicacy, I think!'

Food was very important in Alan's home because they lived in the country and couldn't just pop out to get something. His mum cooked and baked constantly, and indeed still does. Alan used to love her apple pies 'because the pastry had patterns of leaves on it'.

Even now he still craves stovies, which he finds so comforting and often makes in his own home: 'And they also remind me of parties and happy times. I actually really love dishes that are just one thing, instead of lots of different bits to choose from.'

On occasional trips to the chip shop as a child, his preference was always for white pudding suppers over fish suppers – and it still is. 'White pudding rules!' he says.

Touching on dishes he did not like, though, Alan told me: 'I hated celery. My mum used to make celery soup and it made me gag. Nowadays, though, I like celery. But I did learn a lot from watching my mum. I love making soup and hearty things like that, but I pretty much will have a bash at anything, especially in my house in upstate New York, because, like my childhood, it's the kind of place that you have to cook at home because you are up a mountain and there is no other alternative.'

When he returns to Scotland, Alan loves eating white pudding suppers – 'and the seafood always tastes so much better in Scotland. I am getting good at making my own cullen skink too.'

The mention of New Year brings back many happy memories for Alan: 'I used to love the spread that my parents would put out on Hogmanay, a real mix of sandwiches and cake and scones and nuts and all sorts. I do love a smorgasbord!'

Vegetarian Stovies
serves many

Stovies is a Scottish dish that is traditionally made with beef dripping, but I am a vegetarian so I have made up my own version. It is real peasant food and ideal for people who, like me, like to have a plateful of one thing. I much prefer a mush-style dish to something with loads of different components.

Stovies are so great for parties on cold winter nights because you can just leave them on the stove and people can help themselves throughout the night as they please.

olive oil
3–4 cloves of garlic (more, if you like)
4 large onions
8–10 large potatoes

tamari or dark soy sauce, to taste
Worcestershire sauce, to taste
salt and pepper, to taste
a couple of handfuls of soya mince

In a wok or large pot, put a good old sloosh of olive oil. (I normally turn the bottle upside down and count until about four.) Chop up some garlic, and fry it in the olive oil for a bit. Don't let them get crispy, but they need to permeate the oil and make a tasty base for the stovies.

Take the biggish onions and chop them up (fairly big chunks, not that sort of manic onion slush that fancy chefs do) and add them to the olive oil and garlic. Fry them for a bit longer then put a lid on and leave them to sweat for a bit (about 5 minutes).

Now scrub and chop up the potatoes. Chop them into fairly big, mouthful-size chunks. Add the potatoes to the sweating onions and garlic and leave them for a bit to get all infused.

Now comes the fun bit. Get your tamari or dark soy sauce and squirt about 20 or so squirts into the wok, then do the same with your Worcestershire sauce. You could also use BBQ sauce or something like that; basically the trick is to make the stovies tasty and to give it a bit of a browny colour. You do all this to taste, and you can also add some salt and pepper if you like (although don't go crazy with the salt if you are going heavy on the tamari).

Then throw in a couple of big handfuls of the TVP, aka Textured Vegetable Protein (I like to call it soya mince because TVP sounds strange. Rather funnily my assistant, Joey, thought I said soya mints the first time I asked him to buy some and he had a devil of a job tracking any down). The thing with the soya mince is that it swells up in the water and gives the stovies some nice texture and taste and also makes it thicker. So if your stovies are too runny, throw in some more to them thicken up. *Continued overleaf.*

Vegetarian Stovies

continued

Pour water into the wok so that all the ingredients are just submerged. Bring to the boil for a bit, turn it down to simmer, then go away and check your email or have a bath or something. Stir occasionally, and once the potatoes are cooked you can give them a little beating up with a spoon to make the stovies more mushy.

I usually cook mine for about 30 minutes, with the lid half on, half off. Then you can turn them off, put the lid on and let them cook in their own juices.

As you will have noticed, I don't really do precise measurements when I cook. Basically this is a mushy, potato stewy thing that can come in various consistencies and you just have to find the combination that suits you best. You could also add things like hot sauce or mustard if you felt daring. Enjoy!

Sue says: This dish requires no additional salt if you are using both tamari sauce and Worcestershire sauce.

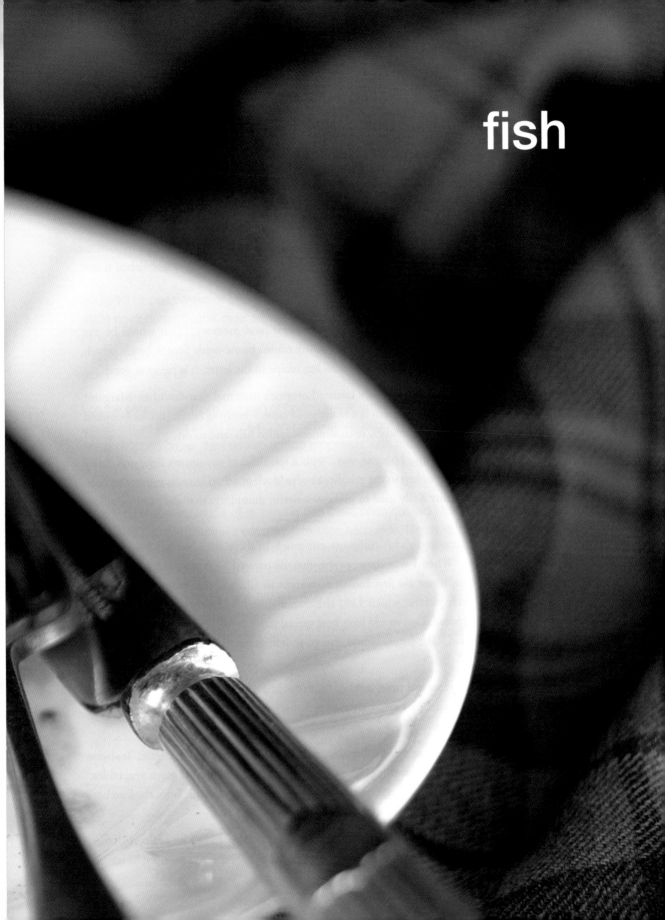

fish

Islay Scallop Salad with Asparagus
serves 3–4

Sue says: My recipe hopefully meets with George's approval.

olive oil, for cooking
12 plump scallops
1 large bag of interesting salad leaves,
    washed

200g/7 oz fine asparagus,
    lightly cooked

For the vinaigrette:
1 tbsp sherry vinegar
½ tsp Dijon mustard
sea salt and freshly ground black
    pepper, to taste

approx. 4 tbsp extra virgin
    olive oil

First, make the vinaigrette. Mix the vinegar and mustard and some sea salt in a small bowl. Using a small whisk, whisk in the oil to make an emulsion. Check the seasoning, adding some black pepper.

Pour 1 tablespoon of oil into a heavy frying pan and heat until very hot. Once it is searing hot (this will take a couple of minutes) add half the scallops (they will spit) and cook for 2–3 minutes, turning after 1 minute, then remove and keep warm. Cook the remaining scallops in more oil, if necessary.

Meanwhile, toss the salad leaves in a bowl with the vinaigrette, then top with the seared scallops and asparagus. Serve with crusty bread.

Kedgeree
serves 6

approx. 680g/1 lb 8 oz long-grain rice
2–3 large fillets smoked haddock, cooked and flaked
6 hard-boiled eggs, peeled and quartered
75g/2¾ oz butter, for cooking

My mum cooked plenty of long-grain rice in a pan of boiling water until it was fluffy then mixed it with cooked, flaked smoked haddock and peeled and quartered hard-boiled eggs. She then melted lots of butter in a pan and gently combined everything – and that was that. Simple, but delicious!

Sue says: Although Gavin's mum's recipe is simply rice, fish, eggs and butter, I like to add some spring onions sautéed in butter, a little curry powder and some cherry plum tomatoes sliced in half.

meat

Overnight Beef Stew

serves 6–8

My mum cooked this often, and it is one of my favourite dishes; she never added the peas but I reckon these make it my own signature dish.

flour, for coating

salt and pepper

1kg/2 lb 4 oz stewing beef (ask your butcher to cut some really good beef for you), cut into cubes

oil, for cooking

2 onions, peeled and chopped

4 carrots, peeled and chopped

2 leeks, chopped

1 small turnip (swede), peeled and chopped

600ml/1 pint fresh beef stock

Dijon mustard

couple of handfuls of frozen peas

Season some flour and place in a large plastic bag with the beef and shake well, to coat. Seal this in a hot pan with a little oil then remove.

Add the onions, carrots, leeks and turnip to the pan and sweat these down. Then transfer these and the meat to a big cast-iron pan. Cover with fresh beef stock, season well and stir in some Dijon mustard. Cover with a lid then place in a low oven, preheated to 150°C/300°F/Gas 2 for at least 4 hours, or overnight.

Once cooked, you can cool the stew then reheat it the next day when it is even better. Then add some frozen peas to the cooked hot stew, heat it until the peas are cooked, then serve it piping hot with some broccoli or French beans and new potatoes tossed in mint and butter.

Steak Pie

serves 6

Sue says: The pie Barbara remembers from New Year was home-made steak pie in a metal pie dish full to the brim with glossy steak with a pie funnel in the centre, covered with yummy puff pastry. This is my version.

50g/1¾ oz dripping or butter
900g/2 lb stewing beef, diced
45g/1½ oz plain flour, seasoned
1 large onion, peeled and chopped
4 large carrots, peeled and cut into
 thick slices

600ml/1 pint beef stock, hot
1 heaped tbsp tomato purée
1 tbsp Worcestershire sauce
salt and pepper, to taste
225g/8 oz ready-rolled puff pastry
1 small free-range egg, beaten

Heat the dripping or butter in a heavy saucepan or casserole. Toss half the meat in the well-seasoned flour, add it to the pan and brown it all over. When browned, remove it with a slotted spoon, coat the remaining meat and brown this batch all over.

Remove with a slotted spoon and add the onion and carrots (if you need it, add a little extra fat at this stage). Gently fry until softened, for about 5 minutes, then return the meat to the pan with the hot stock, tomato purée and Worcestershire sauce. Grind in plenty of black pepper and some salt, stir well and bring to the boil. Cover and reduce to a simmer. Cook very gently for 2 hours, stirring once, then check the seasoning, tip into a 1.8 litre/3 pint pie dish and allow to cool completely. Refrigerate overnight.

Next day, cut a long strip of the rolled-out pastry. Wet your fingers lightly and dampen the edges of the pie dish. Place the pastry strip around the rim of the pie dish, then brush with the beaten egg. Place the remaining pastry over the top as a lid and press down to seal all the edges. Trim off any excess pastry and crimp the edges between thumb and forefinger. Brush with beaten egg and snip a hole – with scissors – in the middle.

Bake in an oven preheated to 220°C/425°F/Gas 7 for 30–35 minutes until puffed up and golden brown. You might need to lightly lay a piece of foil over the surface for the last 10 minutes or so to prevent burning. Serve piping hot.

Haggis-stuffed Chicken
serves 6

1 large oven-ready chicken
½ butcher's haggis

a large handful of chopped dried
    apricots, dates and prunes, and
    some sultanas

I take one large chicken then about half a haggis (I usually buy a Macsweens at the airport on the way back south to England) and heat it through a little so it is easier to handle. I then mix the apricots, dates and prunes, with the sultanas, combine all these with the haggis and stuff this into the chicken.

Then I roast the chicken in an oven preheated to 180°C/350°F/Gas 4 and cook according to its weight (around 20 minutes per 450g/1 lb), giving it a little longer since it is stuffed. Serve the cooked chicken with broccoli and roast carrots, roast parsnips and – my favourite – roast sweet potatoes.

Lamb and Black Pudding Casserole
serves 8

My wife Maggie says, 'This is based on an old navarin of lamb recipe I've used forever, and adapted as the seasons change. Keep a check on the liquid levels. If it's looking too dry, add some water. In winter I've added cooked butter beans instead of new tatties, which makes it lovely and mealie.'

1kg/2 lb 4 oz lamb gigot (leg) chops
1 tbsp flour
2 onions, chopped small
olive oil, for cooking
2 leeks, sliced
1 tsp sugar
200ml/7 fl oz/1 cup wine
400g tin chopped tomatoes or a large
   jar of passata

2 large carrots, peeled and sliced
   (or in summer, 2 handfuls of small
   whole carrots)
1 bay leaf
a couple of sprigs of fresh thyme
   (or 1 tsp dried)
salt and pepper, to taste
8 small new potatoes, sliced thickly
8 slices of Stornoway black pudding
(skinned)
chopped parsley or coriander, to serve

Cut the gigot chops into pieces and toss them in the flour. In an ovenproof casserole, fry off the onions gently in olive oil until softening. Add the leeks and sweat until they are a tangled mass. Remove to a plate. Turn up the heat and brown the lamb in batches. Stir in the sugar, return the onions and leeks to the pan, then stir in the wine and wait until it bubbles. Add the tomatoes or passata. If using old carrots, add them now. Bring to the boil, add the bay leaf and thyme and season to taste. Cook slowly with a lid on the casserole for about 30 minutes – the timing really depends on the age of the lamb – or put it into an oven preheated to 170°C/ 325°F/Gas 3 for about the same length of time.

Remove the lid and add the sliced potatoes (and small carrots in summer). Put back on the hob or in the oven for another 30 minutes.

Meanwhile, place the sliced black pudding on a baking tray in the oven for 15 minutes. The outside will crisp up. Cut into large chunks and add it to the casserole for the last 15 minutes of cooking time.

I strew chopped parsley or coriander on top before serving. It's a really good one-pot meal in the summer. In winter I sometimes omit the new potatoes and serve it with mash.

Sue says: I have also strewn it with rocket instead of parsley or coriander and it works very well.

puddings

Ewan McGregor, actor
born 1971

Ewan McGregor's earliest memories as a child are of eating Scotch pies with his dad while watching the rugby on television. The pies came with gravy and tomato sauce.

Some of the dishes he loved most in his childhood were his mum's beef and Guinness stew, her mince and potatoes and also her tablet. She was – and is – a great cook.

One of Ewan's favourite recipes is his mum's very special bread and butter pudding.

Bread and Butter Pudding
serves 6

butter, for greasing
8 slices of bread, buttered, with
   crusts removed
275ml/9½ fl oz full cream milk
50ml/2 fl oz double cream
3 eggs, slightly beaten

100g/3½ oz caster sugar
110g/4 oz sultanas
½ tsp cinnamon
grated nutmeg, whipped cream
   and fruit, to serve

Preheat the oven to 180°C/350°F/Gas Mark 4 and butter six individual dishes. Line the dishes with the buttered bread.

Add the milk and cream to the eggs and whisk, then whisk in the sugar. Add the sultanas and cinnamon to the egg mixture and pour over the bread, ensuring each slice gets its share of sultanas.

Bake for about 30 minutes or until just set.

Sprinkle with nutmeg, whipped cream and fruit of choice and serve warm.

Muriel Hadden's Cloutie Dumpling
serves 8

Sue says: The word cloth is the origin of this dumpling recipe, as 'cloot' or 'clout' is Scots for cloth, and it refers to the cloth in which the dumpling is boiled. Unlike any other dumplings or steamed puddings, it forms a characteristic 'skin', made by sprinkling flour and sugar into the cloth before filling with the mixture.

The skin must be dried off before serving – done nowadays in the oven, although it used to be done in front of the open fireplace. It was made only for special occasions such as birthdays (in which case there were silver threepennies hidden inside, similar to charms in a Christmas pudding). It would then be eaten with custard. Next day, any leftovers would be served for breakfast: sliced and fried in rendered suet and eaten with bacon.

If you want to add coins, wrap five-pence pieces or charms in waxed or greaseproof paper and add to the mixture. This is my Auntie Muriel's recipe, one of our family's treasures.

225g/8 oz plain flour, sifted
200g/7 oz golden caster sugar
1 level tsp ground cinnamon
1 heaped tsp mixed spice
110g/4 oz shredded suet
110g/4 oz sultanas

110g/4 oz currants
110g/4 oz stoned dates, finely chopped
1 heaped tsp bicarbonate of soda
approx. 200ml/7 fl oz milk, sour milk or
    cold tea
flour and caster sugar, to sprinkle

Mix the first 9 ingredients together in a bowl with enough liquid to make a soft dough of a stiff, dropping consistency.

Dip a large pudding cloth (or tea towel) into boiling water then drain well and lay out flat on a table. Sprinkle with flour and then sugar (I use my flour and sugar shakers): you want an even – but not thick – sprinkling. Place the mixture in the middle of the cloth then tie up the cloth securely with string, allowing a little room for expansion. Place on a heatproof plate in the bottom of a large saucepan. Top up with boiling water to just cover the pudding then cover with a lid and simmer gently for 3¾–4 hours. Check the water level occasionally and top up if necessary. (You should continually hear the reassuring, gentle shuddering sound of the plate on the bottom of the pan for the entire duration of cooking.)

Wearing oven gloves, remove the pudding from the pan, dip briefly into a bowl of cold water: for no more than 10 seconds – so the skin does not stick to the cloth. Cut the string, untie the cloth and invert the dumpling onto an ovenproof plate. Place in an oven preheated to 180°C/350°F/Gas 4 for 10–15 minutes – just until the skin feels less sticky – then sprinkle with caster sugar and serve hot with custard *and* ice cream!

Never-fail Apple Sponge
serves 6

Here's my mum's recipe for her apple sponge, which she got from a little cookery book when she lived in New Zealand, printed by Christchurch West High School.

1.3kg/3 lb cooking apples

2 tbsp sugar

For the sponge:
2 very large eggs (or 3 medium-sized ones)
½ tsp bicarbonate of soda
125g/4½ oz caster sugar

125g/4½ oz plain flour
1 tsp cream of tartar

Peel and core the apples and slice them very thinly, laying them in the bottom of a 23cm/9 in square baking tin. Sprinkle with sugar.

For the sponge, beat the eggs and soda together well. Add the sugar very slowly and beat it in thoroughly (several minutes in a food mixer). Sift in the flour with the cream of tartar and fold in gently.

Pour this mixture over the apples. Put the tin in an oven preheated to 180°C/350°F/Gas 4 for 15–20 minutes until just set.

Sue says: I prefer to cook the apples first in a microwave bowl for a few minutes until just done, then drain off any excess liquid before laying them over the base of the tin.

Gordon Brown, Prime Minister
born 1951

'Growing up in Kirkcaldy, my father was the minister of our local church. This meant that our home, the manse, was always open to visitors. People would call in to speak to my mum and dad about all kinds of local activities to get their support and involvement, or just to have a chat. Everyone was always invited for a cup of tea and sometimes to eat. My mum would always have a huge pot of soup sitting on the stove so there was always something hot and nourishing to offer guests. As one of three boys we had great appetites, so she was also busy making big stews or Sunday roasts served with potatoes and vegetables. I never had a problem eating my greens, and my favourites are probably sprouts because I associate them with my mum's great Christmas roasts. We lived by the sea so we grew up eating lots of fish as well.'

They hardly ever had sweets, but there was always a pudding with their supper and, he says, 'I've never quite given up that habit!' In the summertime, they would go out picking raspberries and would have those with ice cream as a treat. 'My mum was also a great apple crumble and custard person, which we all loved. My dad had to look after the cooking for a long time once while my mother was unwell. He had only one dish that he made: omelettes with cornflour – an ingredient I have never understood for an omelette to this day! But I do remember how hard he tried to make sure that my brothers and I were well fed and looked after in my mother's absence. I'm not much better at cooking myself but I'm OK at rustling up a simple lunch or supper for the boys when needs be, and the microwave is a wonderful invention for when I'm on my own or working late. My father could have done with one of those!'

CAKE

BISCUITS

PASTRY

Apple and Blackberry Crumble

serves 4

175g/6 oz flour (a mixture of brown and white flour is best)
50g/1¾ oz low-fat margarine
50g/1¾ oz butter
50g/1¾ oz soft brown sugar, plus an extra 3 tbsp

2 tbsp muesli (optional)
225g/8 oz cooking apples, peeled, cored and cut into chunks
225g/8 oz blackberries (or rhubarb washed and cut into small chunks, or raspberries in the summer)

Preheat the oven to 200°C/400°F/Gas 6.

Put the flour, margarine and butter into a big mixing bowl and rub together through your fingers until it looks like breadcrumbs. Stir in the 50g/1¾ oz sugar, and for a little extra crunch, add a handful of muesli, if you like.

Load the apple chunks and blackberries (or other fruit) into a pie dish. Sprinkle 3 tablespoons of sugar over the fruit and a tiny dash of water. Pile the crumble mixture over the fruit, smoothing over to make a flat surface without pressing down too hard.

Bake in the oven for about 25 minutes until the crumble top is golden and you can just see the fruit bubbling at the edges.

You can serve the crumble straightaway with custard, yoghurt or ice cream, but it is also good cold if you have any left over the next day.

Sue says: I add an extra 50g/1¾ oz butter to the crumble to make it moist.

bakes

John Barrowman, actor
and musical performer
born 1967

'Oh, I have lots of early food memories,' says John Barrowman about his Glasgow childhood. 'The Barrowmans love their food, especially desserts. I remember a family wedding where everyone, including the bridal party, was already seated to be served dinner and we were still checking out the dessert buffet. You've got to plan your main course around the dessert options. Everyone knows that. Probably my earliest memory, though, is of my Gran Butler – her name was Marion but we called her Murn – making me chips and deep frying Spam slices in her Sandyhills flat. She had the mankiest pot of lard in her cupboard that she recycled for everything fried, so no matter what she made, it tasted really delicious and always had a hint of the flavours of the last foods cooked in the pan. Yum!'

John's mum is a good baker and his other gran, Emily Barrowman, used to make 'the most amazing pancakes; and my sister, Carole, has inherited that skill. In the States we eat them for breakfast and top them with butter, syrup or fresh fruit. When I was a boy, at my Gran Barrowman's on a Sunday she'd make pancakes for lunch and we'd layer them with her home-made jams. Now that I think about it, both my mum and my Gran Barrowman made lots of home-made jams – gooseberry was a family favourite.'

John's mum, also named Marion, would make him a soft-boiled egg with toast cut into thin 'soldiers' for his tea when he was a child, and John told me he still makes a 'boiled egg with soldiers' when he is by himself. He also loves a big American breakfast: waffles or pancakes, eggs, toast, sausages, crunchy bacon and hash browns, which he insists must be crispy round the edges. When he was growing up in America (the family moved to the States in 1976 when he was eight), his mum often cooked a big breakfast on a Saturday morning and he'd stay in bed until he couldn't resist the smells wafting up the stairs.

'When we lived in Scotland, I have memories of eating at friends' and family members' houses pretty regularly, and on Sundays we'd eat a formal lunch at my Gran Barrowman's house. We were usually joined by my cousins and so the food memories are mixed up with memories of playing with them. When we moved to the States, my mum, dad and I and some good friends, who had three girls around my age, would have "Dallas Nights" on Friday nights.

We'd all go out to the Moose Lodge for dinner, usually a cod or perch fish fry, and then we'd come back to our house to eat sweets and watch *Dallas*. That was heaven!'

When I asked John about his preference for a fish or pudding supper from the chip shop, he told me enigmatically, 'I'm a bit like Captain Jack in this regard. I can go either way – fish supper or black pudding!'

He hated tripe as a child: 'No question about it. My mum would stretch the food budget when we were very young and one night a week she'd make tripe with a side of mashed potatoes so we'd have something to soak up the oniony-milky broth the tripe floated in – yes, we would have to finish the broth because 'all the goodness is in the broth. On those nights, we could eat in front of the TV– as if that would make it taste better.'

John grew up around a number of very capable women: 'my mum, Murn, and Murn's sister, Jeannie – and each one could cook. In fact, when I was growing up the kitchen was always the heart of the house. As a result, I love to cook and I'm pretty good at it. When I have time, I do most of the cooking. Fresh salmon is fantastic. Actually, I like to experiment with different ways to cook and dress fish. Of course, I must admit I also love all the things that go along with the art of cooking – the gadgets, the dishes, the utensils, the big shiny pots and pans!'

And as for cooking Scottish dishes, John's niece, Clare, and he have assisted his mum in making cloutie dumpling, a staple for the family's Christmas dinner. 'My mum puts healthy amounts of whisky and brandy in her recipe. I think Clare and I both still need some practice. This is a family food tradition I don't want to lose. There's nothing better after a delicious Christmas dinner than a thick slice of cloutie dumpling swimming in condensed milk or covered in fresh cream. After my mum has wrapped the mixture in the clout, and before she immerses it in the pot of boiling water, everyone in the kitchen has to "slap the dumpling's bum" so it develops a good thick skin. Works every time.'

When he returns to Scotland, John likes to order a fish supper and he always has to buy a supply of Irn-Bru to have on hand for family when they visit him in London or Cardiff.

Recalling special family occasions, he told me about the importance of Hogmanay and New Year's Day, even now. 'At Hogmanay my mum bakes shortbread and we have to greet the New Year with that and slices of Black Bun. Oh, and wee drams of whisky for my dad and not-so-wee glasses of champagne for the rest of us. New Year's Day we have my mum's steak pie with a flaky crust, roast potatoes and Brussels sprouts. Dessert is usually trifle and mince pies. My mouth is watering.'

Banana and Honey Bread

makes one loaf

This is my mum Marion's recipe.

225g/8 oz plain flour
1 tsp baking powder
pinch of salt
115g/4 oz butter, diced
85g/3 oz light brown sugar

200g/7 oz raisins
3 medium-sized ripe bananas
2 tbsp clear/runny honey
2 eggs

Sift together the flour, baking powder and a pinch of salt. Rub in the butter until it resembles breadcrumbs. Stir in the sugar and raisins. Mash the bananas in a separate bowl.

Whisk together the honey and eggs then add this to the dry ingredients, combining well. Pour into a buttered, base-lined loaf tin (900g/2 lb) and bake for 80–90 minutes, covering loosely with foil for the last 30 minutes. Cook until a skewer comes out clean.

Cool in the tin for 5 minutes then remove carefully to a wire rack to cool completely before cutting.

Sue says: This is also delicious served slightly warm as a pudding with honeycomb ice cream and strawberries.

Sticky Gingerbread

makes 1 loaf

This is my Aunt Sheila's recipe; profoundly corrupt and sybaritic people will whack a dod of salty butter onto slices of this gingerbread.

225g/8 oz butter
225g/8 oz soft dark brown sugar
280g/10 oz black treacle
280g/10 oz plain flour
2 tsp ground ginger

1 tsp ground cinnamon
2 large eggs
1 tsp bicarbonate of soda
100ml/3½ fl oz/½ cup milk, warmed

Heat the first 3 ingredients in a pan until liquid.

Meanwhile, sift the flour, ginger and cinnamon into a big bowl. Beat in the eggs. Dissolve the bicarbonate of soda in the warm milk and add this to the mixture. Mix everything together and put it into one or two lined loaf tins.

Cook for 50 minutes–one hour in an oven preheated to 180°C/350°F/Gas 4 (less in a fan oven, obviously), but the only way to reckon it is ready is by the smell! It should sink, with an air of gentle resignation, in the centre, producing a moist effect which is entirely delectable.

Coffee Buns

makes 12

Sue says: Siobhan's sister could not find her old recipe so I tried various ones to come up with the description of both texture and appearance given by Siobhan. Some recipes use soft brown sugar but these, below, are more the right texture which has a hint of a rock bun but not as hard, and also of an American cookie but not as crisp. The presence of coffee in the recipe is mainly for colour so don't worry if you can't taste it. Milk can be used instead of egg to glaze, though egg is traditional as it makes the top glossier. My recipe will hopefully meet with Siobhan's approval.

150g/5½ oz butter, softened
150g/5½ oz unrefined Demerara sugar
1 large egg
15ml (1 tbsp) coffee essence (or 1 tbsp strong black coffee, cooled)

300g/10 oz self-raising flour, sifted
50g/1¾ oz currants
a pinch of salt
1 beaten egg yolk, to glaze

Cream the butter and sugar together. Beat in the egg then the coffee essence. Add in the flour, currants and a pinch of salt then, using your hands, roll into 12 balls.

Place on a greased baking sheet and flatten slightly. Brush the top with the egg yolk then bake in an oven preheated to 190°C/375°F/Gas 5 for about 15 minutes or until golden and just firm.

Remove to a wire rack to cool.

Coconut Balls
makes 18–20

115g/4 oz unsalted butter, softened
115g/4 oz icing sugar, sifted
175g/6 oz desiccated coconut

½ x 400g tin of condensed milk
250–300g/9–10 oz quality chocolate
 (half dark, half milk)

Cream the butter, mix in the sugar, coconut and milk. Mix well and roll into 18–20 balls. Place on greaseproof paper on a baking tray and put it in the fridge for an hour. (Sue says: I place the uncoated balls in the freezer for 20 minutes or so which makes it easier to coat in the chocolate.)

Remove the tray from the freezer, melt the chocolate and, using 2 forks, dip in the coconut balls. Place each chocolate-coated ball on a sheet of greaseproof paper to set.

Gypsy Creams

makes 10

A brief recipe... I'm guessing a bit because the ink's run in my mother's old recipe book and the page is very yellow. Once upon a time I knew it off by heart.

They should be rounded when they come out of the oven and, of course, then be sandwiched together. They don't necessarily look wonderfully attractive – but the taste... Sod Proust and his Madeleines! This is so much better – the taste of a small sweet sin.

55g/2 oz margarine or butter
55g/2 oz lard
55g/2 oz caster sugar
100g/3½ oz/1 cup porridge oats

115g/4 oz/1 cup plain flour
2 tsp cocoa powder
2 tsp syrup
2 tbsp hot water

For the filling:
55g/2 oz margarine or butter
100g/3½ oz icing sugar, sifted

2 tsp cocoa, sifted

Cream the fats and sugar together. Add the porridge oats, flour and cocoa, then the syrup and water. Combine gently then drop teaspoonfuls onto a greased baking sheet (about 20).

Bake in an oven preheated to 180°C/350°F/Gas 4 for 15 minutes. Remove to a wire rack to cool.

Meanwhile, make the filling. Beat together all the ingredients until smooth, then use to sandwich together 2 biscuits.

Sue says: This recipe really does work, even though Sharman 'guessed at it'!

Kaye Adams, broadcaster
born 1962

'My earliest childhood memory is one I told my daughter about... stupidly. I can remember at a very early age making butterballs. Blobs of butter rolled in sugar: and we ate them! My teeth ache at the thought of them now but my five-year-old thinks they sound delicious,' Kaye tells me. And describing how she grew up in Grangemouth, she says, 'We were far from foodies. My mum worked full time and so had no time to experiment or cook for fun, so food was functional. My granny was a very good baker. She made a lovely Victoria sponge and blackberry and apple jelly, which I loved.'

Kaye's favourite childhood dish was mince and tatties; she still craves it, but since nowadays she is a fish-eating vegetarian, it's a bit tricky to eat it! From time to time she makes quorn mince and tatties, but she reckons it's not the same. As a child, she ate out sometimes: 'At Berni Inns we would have prawn cocktail, steak and baked potato followed by Black Forest gâteau.' They also did high tea on a Sunday quite a lot and she recalls 'ploughing through fish and chips and peas just to get to the cakes at the end'.

She loathed liver as a child and tells me just how strong this hatred was: 'At one school I went to, they served it every week and every week I would leave the dining room with a piece of gravy-sodden liver in my blazer pocket. By the end of term, there were living organisms camping in there!'

Nowadays, the most Scottish thing she cooks is lentil soup or Scotch broth (with no meat), as she loves soup. She also loves Scottish shellfish and Arbroath Smokies, but another meaty memory is of Sunday: 'Every Sunday we had a piece of silverside. I've no idea what that is, apart from a lump of beef, but we had it every Sunday in life!'

Millionaire's Shortbread

makes 24 pieces

Sue says: Kaye's friend Shirley Blair's mum was a wonderful baker and Kaye used to watch her make this glorious stuff 'barely able to contain my excitement'. Hopefully my recipe will hit the spot too!

For the shortbread base:
175g/6 oz plain flour
75g/2¾ oz cornflour
75g/2¾ oz golden caster sugar

175g/6 oz slightly salted butter,
   slightly softened

For the caramel and topping:
2 x 400g tins of condensed milk

300g/10½ oz quality chocolate
   (half milk, half plain)

Sift the flours into a food processor, add the caster sugar and then butter, then whiz briefly to bring the mixture together into a ball. Remove from the processor and knead it lightly.

Press the mixture into a lightly greased Swiss-roll tin that is 33cm x 23cm/13 in x 9 in, and press flat. Prick with a fork and bake in an oven preheated to 180°C/350°F/Gas 4 for about 25 minutes or until golden brown. Cool in the tin.

To make the caramel, place the unopened cans of milk on their sides in a heavy saucepan and cover with boiling water; the water should almost cover the tins. Cover and simmer for 2 hours, checking now and then, topping up with more boiling water if necessary. Remove the cans and leave to cool completely before opening and spreading carefully over the base. Leave until cold.

Finally, melt the chocolate then spread it over the caramel. Cut into 24 squares once set.

Sunday Afternoon Drop Scones
(Scotch Pancakes)

makes 24–30

I asked my mother to write out this recipe for me recently because I wanted to make them for my son. She used to make these drop scones for me and my sisters and we would eat them in front of the fire, while watching *The Dukes of Hazzard*. The slightly burnt, sweetish taste is now permanently and oddly associated with law-dodging men in tight denim and noisy cars.

7 dessertspoons plain flour	½ tsp bicarbonate of soda
2 dessertspoons sugar	1 egg
1 tsp cream of tartar	milk

Mix all the dry ingredients together then mix to a thick batter by adding the egg and a few drops of milk.

Drop a few tablespoonfuls of the batter at a time onto a hot, greased girdle, or griddle (or failing that, a frying pan). When golden brown, turn them over and cook them on the other side. They can be kept warm in a tea towel, if you like, but they are actually better eaten as you go along, plain or spread with raspberry jam.

Eyemouth Tart

makes 1 tart

175g/6 oz shortcrust pastry
55g/2 oz currants
55g/2 oz chopped walnuts
55g/2 oz coconut
55g/2 oz glacé cherries, quartered

55g/2 oz raisins
25g/1 oz caster sugar
1 large egg, beaten
25g/1 oz butter, melted

For the topping:
225g/8 oz icing sugar

2 tbsp lemon juice

Roll out the pastry and place in a greased Swiss-roll tin (23cm x 33cm/9 in x 13 in).

Mix all the next 6 ingredients together, add the beaten egg and melted butter and spread over the pastry base. Bake in an oven preheated to 190°C/375°F/Gas 5 for about 25 minutes.

For the topping, mix the icing sugar with the lemon juice and a little water and spread over the top. Cut into squares when cool.

Sue says: The filling was doubled for the photo to make it deeper and even more moist. You can also use different colours of glacé cherries, as we did here.

Chris Paterson, rugby player
born 1978

'My earliest food memory isn't a particularly good one. My main recollection from my early days was that I was a really fussy eater. I can remember sitting at the table in a bad mood picking all the little pieces of onion out of my mince and tatties. I'm happy to say times have changed and I'm no longer a fussy eater. In fact, the opposite.'

Chris Paterson told me that food was important in his home, growing up in Galashiels in the Scottish Borders. 'In our house, however, there was only my mum, dad, me and older brother David and so there was never a mad rush or pile ups to get to the table first. I used to love it when my mum baked at home. I was always very keen to help and lick the spoon! She made great fairy cakes, millionaire's shortbread – and her Christmas cake was baked by November. It was my job between then and Christmas to place slices of bread all round the cake, then re-wrap it. I have no idea why I did this but it was my job. When I removed the bread a week later it was rock hard!' Intrigued by this task (was this a Borders speciality?) I phoned Chris's mum Lyn to ask her about it and she told me it was a tip she had heard on *The Jimmy Young Show* – to put moisture back into the cake if you had overcooked it a little and you felt it might be a little dry. After the bread had been wrapped round the cake for a few days, it was like toast, so the moisture from the bread had gone into the cake. Top tip!

'As for favourite dishes from my childhood – I just wanted to eat whatever was in front of me as quickly as possible so I could then get out and play.' But Chris did tell me that though the food was traditional – stews, mince, soups – it was always good. 'But because I was a really fussy eater as a child, I would never try anything new, so plain fare suited me.' Sunday tea was always roast beef and Yorkshire puddings and New Year was always a steak pie.

'I can remember my granny making porridge with lots of sugar on it: it was great. My grandpa ate his only with salt.' The Patersons had fruit trees in their garden – apple, plum and damson – and Chris's mum would make jam from these, the damson one being a particular favourite.

Chris's granny and grandpa used to take him out for bar suppers quite often. 'We would go out on Saturdays and try new places as often as possible. There was a restaurant in Eddleston, just outside Peebles, which they often took me to when I was probably about seven or eight years old, and I can remember going there and getting my two favourite things: a bowl of cucumber and chips, with salad cream on the side. It was great. I couldn't get it anywhere else!'

Chris, perhaps unusually, hated pizza; 'I must have been the only kid that did. I was never a fan of beef olives either.' But he did always like soups, one of his mum's specials – a chicken and rice broth. His wife Claire also makes fabulous soups now, such as sweet potato and red pepper. His mum tried to teach him how to cook but 'as usual I didn't take too much of it in. Since then TV cooking shows and my wife have been more influential.'

As for producing Scottish dishes to cook now, he often cooks haggis and has porridge most mornings in the winter.

'I think a recipe that would sum up my childhood would be something sweet. I was really bad for only wanting sweet things.' His granny was from Selkirk, although she lived in Galashiels, near Chris's family. 'There was intense rivalry between Gala and Selkirk – most of it tongue in cheek. Into this friendly rivalry came the question of the Selkirk Bannie, which I used to love [it was called 'Selkirk Bannie' in the Borders], since it was loaded with fruit. I would eat that smeared thickly with butter in Galashiels, but with my Selkirk granny!'

Selkirk Bannock

makes 1 large bannock

Sue says: Here is my classic recipe for Chris.

900g/2 lb strong white flour
pinch of salt
2 x 7g sachets of easy-blend dried yeast
55g/2 oz caster sugar
approx. 500ml/18 fl oz semi-skimmed
    milk (or ½ water, ½ milk), warm

150g/5½ oz butter, softened
400g/14 oz sultanas
1 medium free-range egg, beaten,
    to glaze

Sift the flour and a pinch of salt into a bowl, then stir in the yeast and sugar. Add enough warm liquid to combine to a soft but not sticky dough. Turn onto a floured board and knead well for 10 minutes or so until smooth. Place in a bowl, cover and leave somewhere warm for 1–1½ hours, or until well risen.

Cut the softened butter into 4 then fold each piece into the dough, one at a time. Knead until thoroughly amalgamated. Then work in the sultanas, a handful at a time. Shape into a bannock: a round flattened dome about 28cm/11 in in diameter. Place on a buttered baking sheet and leave for about an hour, or until well risen.

Brush with the beaten egg to glaze, then bake in an oven preheated to 220°C/425°F/Gas 7 for 15 minutes. Reduce to 190°C/375°F/Gas 5 and continue to bake for 25–30 minutes, covering loosely with foil for the last 15–20 minutes to prevent the top burning. It is ready once it is golden brown all over and the base sounds hollow when tapped underneath. Leave to cool on a wire rack then slice and spread with butter.

Nairn, Nick 86-7
Naughtie, James 202
Neep Bree 24
Nelson, Nell 168
nuts
    Beef and Chestnut Stew 97
    Black Bun 169
    Eyemouth Tart 200

oats, oatmeal
    Flapjacks 181
    Gypsy Creams 178
    Melting Moments 183
    Mince and Tatties 91
    Porridge 43
O'Farrell, Maggie 190-1
Orkney Dumpling 133

parsnips
    Scotch Broth 16
pasta
    Blue Cheese Pasta 57
    Macaroni Cheese 51
Paterson, Bill 44-5
Paterson, Chris 204-5
Patey, William 114
peas
    Overnight Beef Stew 94
    Scallops with Black Pudding and
        Buster Peas 65
pheasant
    Roast Pheasant 117
pork
    Meatloaf 87
Porridge 43
potatoes
    Alligator Stew 89
    Cullen Skink 28
    Fish Supper 74-5
    Greek Shepherd's Pie 85
    Haggis, Neeps and Tatties 115
    Invalid's Cullen Skink 31
    Lamb and Black Pudding
        Casserole 122
    Lamb Curry 125
    Lentil and Ham Hock Soup 9
    Mince and Tatties 91

Roast Chicken for Sunday
    Dinner 109
Stovies 105
Tattie Scones 46
Tattie Soup 20
Vegetable Soup 19
Vegetarian Stovies 59-60
Pryde, Bill 30-1

Ramsay, Gordon 42-3
Rankin, Ian 18-19
Redmond, Siobhan 162-3
rice
    Chicken Soup with Rice 38
    Home-made Chicken Soup 33
    Kedgeree 78
Robertson, George
    (Lord Robertson of Port Ellen) 66-7

Salmond, Alex 26-7
scallops
    Islay Scallop Salad with
        Asparagus 68
    Scallops with Black Pudding and
        Buster Peas 65
scones
    Buttermilk Fruit Scones 203
    Sunday Afternoon Drop Scones 192
    Tattie Scones 46
    Wholemeal Cheese Scones 25
Scotch Broth 16
Scotch Pancakes 192
Scott, Dougray 92-3
Scott, Tavish 118-19
Scottish Rarebit 53
Selkirk Bannock 206
Shortbread 189
    Millionaire's Shortbread 186
Smillie, Carol 32
Smith, Elaine C. 108
smoked fish
    Cullen Skink 28
    Kedgeree 78
    Smoked Haddock Pie 81
soups
    Bacon, Lentil and Kale Soup 13
    Chicken and Lemon Soup 35

Chicken Soup with Rice 38
Cullen Skink 28
Home-made Chicken Soup 33
Invalid's Cullen Skink 31
Lentil and Ham Hock Soup 9
Neep Bree 24
Scotch Broth 16
Spicy Lentil Soup 11
Tattie Soup 20
Vegetable Soup 19
Spear, Shirley 22-3
spinach
    Smoked Haddock Pie 81
Spiteri, Sharleen 34-5
Stark, Edi 172-3
Steel, Sir David 52
Stovies 105
    Vegetarian Stovies 59-60
Sturgeon, Nicola 12

Tablet 197
Tattie Scones 46
Tattie Soup 20
tomatoes
    Alligator Stew 89
    Bacon, Lentil and Kale Soup 13
    Greek Shepherd's Pie 85
    Lamb and Black Pudding
        Casserole 122
    Lamb Curry 125
    Smoked Haddock Pie 81
    Tomato Sauce 55
turnip (swede)
    Haggis, Neeps and Tatties 115
    Neep Bree 24
    Overnight Beef Stew 94
    Stovies 105
    Vegetable Soup 19

Ure, Midge 56-7

Wark, Kirsty 54
White, Jason 110-11

Young, Kirsty 8-9